SET APART

**30 DEVOTIONS ABOUT HOW
GOD'S GOODNESS CHANGES US**

ISBN 978-1-0877-4439-1
Item 005831827
Dewey Decimal Classification Number: 242
Subject Heading: DEVOTIONAL LITERATURE / BIBLE STUDY AND TEACHING / GOD

Printed in the United States of America

Student Ministry Publishing
LifeWay Resources
One LifeWay Plaza
Nashville, Tennessee 37234

We believe that the Bible has God for its author; salvation for its end; and truth, without any mixture of error, for its matter and that all Scripture is totally true and trustworthy. To review LifeWay's doctrinal guideline, please visit www.lifeway.com/doctrinalguideline.

publishing team

Director, Student Ministry
BEN TRUEBLOOD

Manager, Student Ministry Publishing
JOHN PAUL BASHAM

Editorial Team Leader
KAREN DANIEL

Writer
MIKE LOVATO

Content Editor
KYLE WILTSHIRE

Production Editor
BROOKE HILL

Graphic Designer
JON RODDA

04
intro

05
getting started

06
what is
goodness?

20
are people
naturally good?

36
what does
goodness
look like?

58
what does God say
is good?

72
articles and
resources

table of contents

Intro

Good. We hear the word every day. He's good at basketball. She's a good driver. He's good at drawing. She's good at math. We connect "good" to things that aren't even alive. It was a good movie. The pancakes were really good. That candle smells good. The air conditioner feels good. Sometimes, we even hear the word associated with behavior. She's so good for that teacher. He's good to go over and help that person. We know what is meant when it comes to the word good. But, do we really know what "good" is?

Truth be told, our standard for "good" can often be pretty low. Sometimes the "good" guy in a movie is guilty of doing things that are just as bad as the bad guy. But because we see the story unfold through his or her eyes, we decide what he or she does is good... or at least ok. Other times, something gets labled good simply because it's better than something awful. Like when someone feels good about passing along only a "tiny" bit of gossip, instead of the "big" rumor they heard going around about someone else.

Let's face it: our understanding of good is all over the place. To be honest, there are times when it might even be really confusing to know what really is good. If you feel this way, you're not alone. The world is a confusing place. There are mixed messages coming at you at a million miles an hour all day long. Thankfully, there is an anchor we can hold on to in this storm. There is a standard for what good actually is that we can compare everything else to to see if it really is good.

For the next 30 days, we're going to dive into this concept of goodness. We're going to answer questions like, "What is goodness?", "Are people good?", and "What does goodness really look like?". Ultimately, we will discover not only what goodness is, but who is good, how we can live a life that resembles His, and seek to live in His goodness as well.

getting started

This devotional contains 30 days of content, broken down into sections. Each day is divided into three elements—discover, delight, and display—to help you answer core questions related to Scripture.

discover

This section helps you examine the passage in light of who God is and determine what it says about your identity in relationship to Him. Included here is the daily Scripture reading, focus passage, along with illustrations and commentary to guide you as you explore God's Word.

delight

In this section, you'll be challenged by questions and activities that help you see how God is alive and active in every detail of His Word and your life.

display

Here's where you take action. Display calls you to apply what you've learned through each day's study.

prayer

Each day also includes a prayer activity in one of the three main sections.

Throughout the devotional, you'll also find extra articles and activities to help you connect with the topic personally, such as Scripture memory verses, additional resources, and quotes from leading Christian voices.

DAY 1

GOOD FRUIT

- -

discover |

READ GALATIANS 5:22-23.

But the fruit of the Spirit is love, joy, peace, patience, kindness, goodness, faithfulness, gentleness, and self-control. The law is not against such things.

The people God used to write Scripture often utilized language from nature and agriculture. Picture an apple tree in your mind and imagine what its fruit looks like. They look like apples, right? You'd never go check an orange tree in an attempt to pick some apples.

Paul, as he wrote to the Christians in Galatia, described the type of fruit that results from walking in the Spirit. He listed nine qualities that come about as we are led by the Holy Spirit. An apple tree will produce apples if it's in the right environment (the right temperature and the right type of soil) and has the right resources (sunlight and water). Christians produce the fruit of the Spirit when they place themselves in the right environment (fellowship with God and believers) and have the right resources (Bible intake, prayer, and other disciplines).

Let's zero in on just one fruit mentioned in this passage—goodness. The type of goodness mentioned here is one of moral and spiritual excellence. Goodness shows up in our lives when we choose to slow down and meet the need of a friend who is hurting. Goodness is on display when we reflect God's character by the attitude we show to members of our family.

The reality is that we can only see this type of moral and spiritual excellence in our lives because of the new life we have in Jesus. Today, focus on how the fruit of goodness is visible to those you're around each day.

delight |

How have you seen goodness lived out in the lives of your Christian friends?

How have you seen the Holy Spirit developing goodness as part of His fruit in your life?

display |

Goodness is a quality that has to be lived out. You can't just focus on goodness being present on the inside. Ask yourself a tough question: Would most of my friends describe goodness as a characteristic of my life? After reflecting on that question, take some time this week to intentionally pursue goodness in the way you treat different people in your life. You might seek to pursue goodness with your teachers, your parents, or maybe a difficult person at school.

Take a few minutes to pray. Ask God to reveal to you the areas of your life where goodness is lacking. Ask God to begin transforming those areas of your life. Don't worry about accomplishing this through your own effort. Instead, focus on walking in the Spirit to allow Him to produce this fruit in you.

DAY 2

DEFINER OF GOODNESS

- -

discover |

READ 1 CHRONICLES 16:34.

Give thanks to the LORD, for he is good; his faithful love endures forever.
—1 Chronicles 16:34

What makes someone good? Maybe you've seen them pick up
trash after lunch, befriend someone everyone else avoids, or help
an old lady cross the street. It may seem easy to define goodness,
but in order to fully understand it, we must get to the core of where
goodness comes from.

Yesterday, we talked about how goodness is moral and spiritual
excellence. The reality is that there is only One being who can
determine what is truly good. God is the essence of goodness.
He gets to define goodness because He's both Creator and the
only One in the universe who is fully good. Without God, there is
no good. Any goodness accomplished by people serves as a clue
to the truth that there is indeed a Creator. Humans reflect just a
glimpse of the goodness found in Him.

In 1 Chronicles 16:34, we find a portion of King David's song
of praise, which he commanded to be sung after the ark of the
covenant had been returned to Jerusalem following the defeat of
the Philistines. David's exuberant thanksgiving flowed from a place
of recognizing the goodness of God.

It's reassuring to know that God not only commands goodness to
be displayed in His followers, but to also realize that goodness is
an essential part of God's character. He can only do good; He will
never commit evil. Dwell on the reality today that God is good all
the way to the very center of who He is.

delight |

Why is it such a big deal that God is the ultimate Author of goodness?

Imagine for a moment if God was not truly good. How would that affect other aspects of the Christian faith?

display |

Think for a moment about how you've viewed goodness in the world we live in. Have you defined it by popular opinion or by God's character? Maybe you've somehow mentally separated the good deeds people do from the One who gave them the ability to accomplish them.

Focus your attention today on our God who defines goodness simply because of who He is. He is worthy of your praise and adoration. Pause for a personal time of worship. Focus in on different aspects of God's character. Recognize His goodness in everything He has done.

Stop for a moment and praise God for His goodness. First, praise Him because He is good. Then, thank Him specifically for the ways you've seen Him be good in your life or the lives of others you know. Pray that you would seek to have a heart that looks like His.

DAY 3

GOOD GIFTS

- -

discover |

READ JAMES 1:13-18.

*Every good and perfect gift is from above, coming down from the
Father of lights, who does not change like shifting shadows.*
—James 1:17

My two daughters love to play the blame game with each other.
I'll hear shrieking from another part of the house leading me to
investigate what's going on. Often, both girls are pointing at each
other while simultaneously claiming, "She did it!" Humans have
been playing the blame game since the very beginning. In the
Garden of Eden, Adam blamed Eve, and Eve blamed the serpent
(Gen. 3:12-13).

We still play this blame game today. It's tough to own up to what
you've done! The temptation may even exist at times to blame
God for the times we choose to do evil. James quickly tears this
idea down in the first chapter of his letter. It's impossible for God
to tempt you. Why? Because God isn't tempted by evil and doesn't
tempt anyone else with evil. He is one hundred percent good
without any mix of evil. God's character will never allow for this
type of temptation to come from Him.

James contrasts this with a much better truth: every good thing
comes from God. Evil is not from God; He brings every good thing
into our lives. The difficult truth is that we're the ones to blame
when we choose to sin. The desire comes from within. Today, let
go of any blame you may be holding onto and, instead, choose to
receive the good gifts coming from the Father.

delight |

Do you ever find yourself thinking that perhaps God is tempting you with evil? Why or why not?

What are some ways you've played the blame game when it comes to sin in your life?

display |

One of the most freeing things in our lives is when we own up to our own shortcomings, mistakes, and sins. You'll never be perfect until you reach heaven, so there's no point in trying to play the blame game. You might want to blame God, your friends, or your circumstances, but at the end of the day, the only one to blame for your sin is yourself.

Freedom comes when we stop playing the blame game, own up to what we've done, and experience the refreshment of forgiveness that only Jesus can offer. Choose today to let go of sin and blame. Walk in freedom instead. If you've been blaming someone else for sin in your life, choose today to take responsibility for your own actions.

Reflect on your heart for a few minutes. Ask God to reveal any areas of sin or blame that you may be holding on to. Release those areas to Him as you turn from them and receive forgiveness in their place.

DAY 4

SAVED FOR GOOD WORKS

- -

discover |

READ EPHESIANS 2:1-10.

For you are saved by grace through faith, and this is not from yourselves; it is God's gift—not from works, so that no one can boast. For we are his workmanship, created in Christ Jesus for good works, which God prepared ahead of time for us to do.
—Ephesians 2:8-10

You cannot be good on your own. In fact, the apostle Paul wrote to a church in a city called Ephesus telling them they were dead before Christ. There is no possible way for a person who is dead to be good.

Fortunately for us, Christ has taken spiritually dead people and brought them to life. Jesus brings about the ability for goodness to be present in our lives. It's all because of God's grace, which is activated by our faith—simply placing our trust in what Jesus has done and choosing to follow Him.

There is no amount of good behavior on your part that will move you from being spiritually dead to alive. It is purely a gift from God. If good works saved you, every Christian would end up in a bragging contest about the good things they did to earn salvation.

We are not saved by good works, but we are saved for good works. God saved you so that you can now live in a way that brings goodness into the world all around you. Today, look for opportunities to display how good God has been to you by living out goodness in your life.

delight |

What is the difference between being saved by good works and being saved for good works?

Why do you think some people believe their goodness can save them?

display |

It's really great news that your goodness doesn't save you. You could never be good enough! Even though we know this truth, sometimes we may find ourselves slipping back into a mode of thinking that it's somehow our goodness that keeps us in a right relationship with God. Ask yourself this question: Am I relying on my goodness to save me or am I relying on Jesus to save me?

Cling to the reality that Jesus has accomplished the act of bringing goodness into your life. He sees you as His workmanship. You're an incredible work of art that He's creating to display His goodness. Choose today to live out the good works He's saved you for.

> **Pause for a moment in prayer. Thank God for saving you by grace and not because of any goodness you've been able to accomplish. Praise Him that He has brought you from death to life. Ask Him to show you the good works He's calling you to right now.**

TASTE OF GOODNESS

- -

discover |

READ PSALM 34:8-10.

*Taste and see that the LORD is good. How happy
is the person who takes refuge in Him!*
—*Psalm 34:8*

I remember the first time I ate dinner at a Brazilian churrascaria. I had no idea what I was in for as the servers came by the table with large servings of meat on swords. They would carve off delicious morsels. The best part was that the meat kept coming out as long as the small wooden indicator on our table stayed turned on its green side rather than its red side. I didn't realize certain flavors existed until that meal.

There are some things you can only truly discover by experience. It may be a delicious meal, a view of the mountains, or the breeze of the ocean. You may think you understand by a description or picture, but only experience brings true understanding.

God's goodness is like that. You can read about God's goodness or hear people share their stories of God's goodness, but until you experience it for yourself, you don't truly comprehend it. One small taste of God's goodness leaves you with the reality of how good He truly is.

My first taste of Brazilian barbecue left me wanting more (and probably ended with a stomach ache). But those who taste of God's goodness end up having everything they need and more. Think about the small tastes of God's goodness you've experienced and how they can shape your actions today.

delight |

What are some ways you've tasted God's goodness?

Have you ever tasted God's goodness but still lived as if you hadn't? Why or why not?

display |

Psalm 34:8-10 goes on to mention two key actions we ought to embrace once we've tasted the Lord's goodness. First, we are to fear Him. This essentially means to take God seriously. Second, we are to seek Him. This indicates an intentional pursuit that we put effort into. Hopefully, you've gotten a taste of God's goodness. If so, think about the current status of your fear of the Lord. Also, reflect on the actions you're currently taking to seek God. The taste of God's goodness is motivation to pursue Him with your whole heart.

In your time of prayer, ask God to give you a fresh taste of His goodness today. Ask Him to show you clearly how He's bringing good things into your life. Take time as you pray to engage with God in a serious way that shows your desire to seek Him in every area of your life.

GOD'S GENEROSITY

- -

discover |

READ MATTHEW 20:1-16.

*Don't I have the right to do what I want with what is
mine? Are you jealous because I'm generous?*
—Matthew 20:15

"It's not fair." Most of us learned how to use this phrase pretty early
in life. We hate it when it seems like someone else is benefiting
when we think it ought to be us. Jesus used the parable of the
vineyard workers to display how the distribution of God's goodness
and generosity is up to Him alone. The workers hired earliest
believed they ought to be paid higher wages than those who
worked less, even though they had agreed upon an amount of pay
at the start of the day.

Jealousy of God's goodness has no place in the life of a believer.
Ultimately, God gives the same gift of salvation to everyone who
comes to Him in faith, no matter when or how that happens. You
might find yourself tempted to be jealous when observing a new
believer's influence, giftedness, or perceived blessings. We can
fight this type of jealousy by reminding ourselves that the decision
to give good things to people comes from God alone.

If you hold on to this type of jealousy, there's a scary lie you're
believing: the lie that you know better than God. God alone saves
people. God alone blesses people. And God alone decides what
He gives to His children. Today, reject the lie that you know better
than God and embrace a grateful heart for all the goodness He has
brought to you.

delight |

Why do you think it bothered the workers in the parable that the people hired later got paid the same wage?

Have you ever found yourself jealous of the blessings God has given to someone else? If so, why?

display |

Jealousy is an easy sin to slide into. At our very core, we are constantly telling ourselves a message that says, "I deserve better." What would it look like if, instead of jealousy, you decided to live gratefully because of the incredible gift of salvation God has given you? God's goodness is on display as He decides to generously dispense His goodness.

The response of gratitude requires making the decision to set aside jealous thoughts and being grateful for the brothers and sisters God has brought into His family in different ways. Choose to celebrate their successes and blessings.

Spend a few moments in a prayer of gratitude. Thank God specifically for the ways He has shown His goodness to you. Thank Him for the goodness of both His character and His actions. Thank Him for the other Christians you know and the ways He has drawn them into a relationship with Himself.

EPHESIANS 2:8-10

For you are saved by grace through faith, and this is not from yourselves; it is God's gift—not from works, so that no one can boast. For we are his workmanship, created in Christ Jesus for good works, which God prepared ahead of time for us to do.

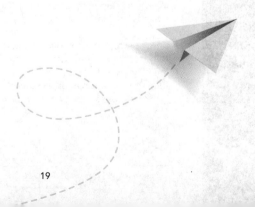

DAY 7

NO ONE IS GOOD

discover |

READ ROMANS 3:9-20.

As it is written: There is no one righteous, not even one. There is no one who understands; there is no one who seeks God. All have turned away; all alike have become worthless. There is no one who does what is good, not even one.
—Romans 3:10–12

In your mind, picture the meanest person you know. Think about the way he or she treats others and how he or she conducts him-or-herself. Now, picture the nicest person you know. Imagine his or her behavior toward other people. Do you know what these two people have in common? Neither of them are truly good. The Bible tells us that no one is righteous, not even the person who seems good by our human standards (we'll talk more about this tomorrow).

Goodness is a fruit of the Spirit. The only way for goodness to truly be in our lives is through the Holy Spirit's work. Apart from this, we constantly turn to our own evil desires and don't produce the goodness God desires. Ever since Adam and Eve first sinned, the human condition is one of sinfulness and evil.

But the recognition of this bad news is what makes the gospel truly good news. Our inability to be good on our own highlights the incredible work of God as He makes us righteous and good through Jesus. Today, allow yourself to sit with the weight of our lack of goodness apart from God's work.

delight |

As you look through today's passage, what thoughts or emotions come to your mind and heart?

If no one is good, how can anyone ever come into a relationship with God?

display |

It's normal to want to think of yourself as better than you really are. No one wants to focus on the bad things he or she does, the dark desires in his or her heart, or the tempting thoughts he or she has. But the Bible makes it clear that none of us are truly good at our core.

The only way we obtain goodness is by the Spirit's work. Perhaps you need to allow the Holy Spirit to begin transforming your life by placing your trust in Jesus for the first time. Or maybe your next step is seeking to walk in step with the Spirit, allowing Him to produce goodness in your life.

> **Allow yourself some quiet space for prayer. Take a moment to realize the utter lack of goodness in your life apart from Christ. Ask God to reveal to you the areas of your life in which you need the Spirit to work and produce goodness. Rest in the fact that your own goodness could never save you, but the goodness of Jesus is more than enough.**

DAY 8

CAPABLE OF GOOD

- -

discover |

READ MATTHEW 7:7-12.

If you then, who are evil, know how to give good gifts to your children, how much more will your Father in heaven give good things to those who ask him.
—Matthew 7:11

Have you ever kept asking your parents for something? Maybe it was for a new phone, a later curfew, or just some cash to hang out with your friends. I'm guessing that you got different answers at different times. Sometimes you ask and they immediately give you what you've asked for. At other times, you may ask for something and it's a firm "no." And yet at other times, they may delay their response because they know it's not the best thing for you right at that moment.

But there's one thing I'm pretty confident about. You probably don't ask for a new phone and receive a rock, a later curfew and receive a 4 p.m. bedtime, or some cash and receive some leftover printer paper. Jesus made a similar point in this parable in Matthew 7. Even though His listeners were evil, they knew how to give good gifts to their children.

You might wonder how an evil person is capable of doing anything good at all. We have all been created in God's image, which gives us the capability for good actions even though we are not naturally good because of the effect of sin on our lives. God, in His infinite goodness, gives much better gifts than what we could ever imagine. Today, focus on the glimpse of goodness we see in humanity because everyone was made in God's image.

delight |

Where have you seen glimpses of goodness in our world?

What do these glimpses of goodness tell us about God's ultimate goodness?

display |

We have been created in God's image (see Gen. 1:26-27). This image has been broken because of sin, but even that broken image reflects some of who God is. His goodness is present in the world even as broken human beings attempt to do what is right.

Make it your goal today to look for these glimpses of God's goodness. Use those glimpses to point people to who God is. Perhaps you'll be able to have a conversation about the gospel as you help someone connect the dots between our attempts at goodness and God's ultimate goodness.

> Spend some time in prayer. Ask God to bring people into your path who need to be pointed to His goodness. Ask God to give you eyes to see the moments when people reflect His image, even if it's a broken attempt. Thank God that His goodness is so much better than our own.

GOD'S GOOD LOVE

- -

discover |

READ ROMANS 5:6-11.

*But God proves his own love for us in that while
we were still sinners, Christ died for us.*
—Romans 5:8

In our culture, we aren't always great at sacrificing for others.
We have a tendency to focus on what's best for ourselves and
not spend too much effort giving up what we want so that others
can benefit. So, can you imagine making an intentional choice to
sacrifice for someone else who doesn't even treat you well?

That's exactly what God did when He sent Jesus to die for you. It's
important to realize that Jesus didn't die for you because of some
sort of goodness you possess. He died for you in spite of your lack
of goodness. One of the most beautiful aspects of the gospel is
that Jesus made the seemingly illogical choice to die for sinners
who didn't deserve it.

Jesus died for His enemies, which gives us a huge reason to
celebrate and rejoice. He knew we desperately needed a Savior
and He was willing to make the ultimate sacrifice on our behalf.
Today, focus on how God reinforces His goodness and love for us
through the death of Jesus even though we didn't deserve it.

delight |

According to Romans 5:8, what did God do to prove His love for us?

How does this prove His love for us?

display |

It wasn't our goodness that caused Jesus to die on our behalf. It was completely an act of God's goodness. God's character moved Him to action when we didn't deserve that action. This act of love ought to motivate us to engage more intentionally in our journey to follow Jesus. After all, it seems pretty ungrateful to live for yourself when Jesus died for you unconditionally.

God's love in this way also motivates us to love others who don't deserve to be loved. We don't love them because of their goodness, but instead we love them because of God's goodness and how He has extended His love to us. Choose today to love someone who doesn't tend to show love to you first.

> **Spend a few moments in prayer. Thank God that He didn't wait for you to be good before sending Jesus to die for you. Sit in a quiet moment of humility as you reflect on how Jesus' dying for you is motivated out of God's great goodness and love. Commit to extend that same type of love to others.**

GOOD FOR NOTHING?

- -

discover |

READ MATTHEW 19:16-22.

Just then someone came up and asked him, "Teacher, what good must I do to have eternal life?" "Why do you ask me about what is good?" he said to him. "There is only one who is good. If you want to enter into life, keep the commandments."
—Matthew 19:16-17

It's a great feeling when you work hard and earn a reward as a result of that hard work. You know what I'm talking about. It's those moments when you put in the extra time at practice and it pays off in the game. Or the moment when you studied extra and bumped your grade up a notch. If we're honest, much of life works this way—except for when it comes to our goodness before God. When we try to apply that same principle of hard work to earn God's approval, it simply falls flat.

God is the only one who is good. There is no amount of human goodness that can bring about eternal life. Jesus encountered this rich young ruler who was eager to discover how he could earn eternal life through his accomplishments. He ultimately walked away sad because, while he indeed kept the commandments, his goodness didn't extend out to every area of his life—most clearly displayed in his love for great wealth.

You'll never be good enough on your own. You can stop trying to play that game. Instead, focus today on how God's goodness is the only way for you to gain eternal life.

delight |

Why do you think many people assume that their good actions will earn them eternal life?

Why are your good efforts not enough to earn God's approval?

display |

The goodness Jesus called us to is an all-in commitment. We can't make this commitment in our own strength. We need the power of the Holy Spirit to save us and transform us. Think about this: Do you view your relationship with God as relying on your own goodness or on the goodness He provides?

Our thinking and actions have a tendency to slip back into a mode of being about our own good actions. Allow God to transform you through His goodness rather than your own. Be honest with yourself and others about your weaknesses and limitations. Embrace what God wants to do in you as you yield to Him.

Rest in this time of prayer. Admit to God that you don't have it all together. You'll never be good enough to earn His approval. But at the same time, thank God that His goodness is enough for you. Praise Him for the eternal life He's given you.

GOOD SOIL

- -

discover |

READ LUKE 8:4-8, 11-15.

But the seed in the good ground—these are the ones who, having heard the word with an honest and good heart, hold on to it and by enduring, produce fruit.
—Luke 8:15

Have you ever heard your parents tell you something they'd like you to do, but because you weren't really listening, you had no idea what they just said after they finished talking? There is a big difference between hearing and truly listening. It's one thing to hear your parents tell you take out the trash, but it's a different thing to actually listen and take out the trash.

The parable of the sower talks about four different types of soil. Each type of soil responds differently to the seed thrown on it. Good soil represents an honest and good heart, which hears the Word, holds on to it, and endures. Ultimately, this is what produces fruit in our lives.

Do you feel like it's a struggle in your life to see spiritual fruit produced? Perhaps there's some work to be done on the condition of the "soil" of your heart. Today, use this time to reflect on how your heart can be more receptive as you receive God's Word. God wants to speak to you through the Bible, but it's essential that you listen with a heart that's ready to receive what He has to say.

delight |

How have you observed different people responding in different ways to the message of the gospel?

What are some things that keep you from being "good soil"?

display |

It's time for a hearing check-up for your heart. We all need the occasional check-up. The parable we've looked at today contains three key components that we see in hearts that are truly ready to hear God's Word. Pick one of these to work on today. First, the heart is honest and good. This means preparing yourself each day to hear from God in a fresh way rather than just going through the motions. Second, the heart holds on to the truth it hears. Are you capturing what God says to you in a journal or some other method? Do you spend time throughout the day remembering what you've heard from God? Finally, the heart endures. We can't hear things from God's Word and then do nothing with it. We must put it into practice on a consistent basis.

Spend a few minutes in prayer. Ask God to reveal to you any areas of your heart that might be blocking you from truly being receptive to His Word. This might be a pattern of sin, a lack of intentional listening, or an unwillingness to put truth into action. Commit to listening with a fresh, good heart.

DAY 12

GOOD THINGS TO COME

---

discover |

READ HEBREWS 10:1-4.

*Since the law has only a shadow of the good things to come, and not
the reality itself of those things, it can never perfect the worshipers
by the same sacrifices they continually offer year after year.*
—*Hebrews 10:1*

The animated classic *Peter Pan* introduces the title character in a
scene in which he has lost his shadow and is searching for it in the
Darling childrens' bedroom. He chases it all over the room before
finally catching it and reattaching it to himself. We laugh at the idea
of a shadow being something that lives on its own, but the reality is
that your shadow only exists because you do.

The author of Hebrews used this imagery of a shadow when
describing the Law in relationship to Jesus. The Old Testament
Law was good, but it was never enough on its own. Jesus is better.
He is "the good things to come." The Law is great at reminding
people of their sin, but not enough to save people from their sin.

What does this mean for us today? It means all your best religious
activity will never be enough to save you. At the end of the day,
apart from Jesus, these types of efforts only point toward your
need for a Savior.

delight |

What role does the Old Testament Law play in the life of a Christian?

How does knowing that the sacrifice Jesus made was permanent and enough to cover every sin you've ever committed or will commit make you feel?

display |

You may be in one of two places today with two different opportunities to live out what you've learned.

- Maybe you've never started a personal relationship with Jesus. As you read the Law discussed in the Bible, it only serves as a huge notice that you've sinned and need a Savior. If that's you, today's a great day to place your trust in Jesus and receive Him as Savior and Lord of your life.

- Maybe you're already a follower of Jesus, but you've allowed yourself to live in a way that attempts to see the Law as your means of earning God's approval. If that's you, reject the thinking that the Law will make you righteous and remind yourself that only Jesus can do this.

Pray today that you would keep Jesus at the center of your heart and mind. Allow yourself to be reminded of your need for a Savior as you think about the sin that may have recently crept into your life. Give those sins to Jesus, because only He can forgive and bring true life.

DAY 13

A GOOD MAN

- -

discover |

READ ACTS 11:19-26.

For he was a good man, full of the Holy Spirit and of faith.
And large numbers of people were added to the Lord.
—Acts 11:24

What makes someone good? If only God is good, why is Barnabas
described as good in Acts 11? Barnabas's goodness came not from
himself, but rather from God. Barnabas is described as being full
of the Holy Spirit and of faith. His status as a good man is solely
because of God's work in him through the Holy Spirit.

The Holy Spirit was Barnabas's source of his goodness, and the
result of this goodness was the encouraging and equipping of the
young church at Antioch. It gave Barnabas incredible joy to see
what God was doing at Antioch. He encouraged the church to stay
strong in its commitment to God, and he also brought in Paul to
teach and equip these new disciples.

God can do an amazing work through you when you pursue Him
and desire the goodness He can bring into your life. The Lord
can empower you to be characterized by goodness and can use
you to encourage and equip other followers of Jesus as well. Your
role is to choose daily to be filled by the Holy Spirit as you walk
through life.

delight |

What are some characteristics of a good person according to the Scripture you read today?

Who is a Christian you would describe as good? What makes you describe them that way?

display |

You will never be able to live out the Christian life through your own power. It's simply impossible. Many students struggle to walk with God because they're trying to do it on their own strength. Choose today to allow God to transform you into a person of goodness. Is your time with God a priority in your life? Is it something you do if you end up with time in your schedule or is it part of your day no matter what happens?

One motivation to help you pursue walking with God daily is when you picture how He may use you for His kingdom work. Imagine the exciting things God wants to do through you as you encourage other believers, share the gospel with non-believers, and help other people grow in their faith.

> **Spend a few moments in prayer. Ask God to give you a fresh desire for His goodness. Ask Him to fill you with His Spirit. Confess any times you've tried to live as a Christian through your own power. Submit your day and your desires to Him.**

LUKE 6:45

A good person produces good out of the good stored up in his heart. An evil person produces evil out of the evil stored up in his heart, for his mouth speaks from the overflow of the heart.

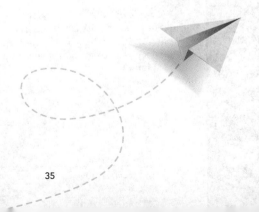

DAY 14

THE GOOD OF OTHERS

- -

discover |

READ ROMANS 15:1-6, 14.

Each one of us is to please his neighbor for his good, to build him up.
—Romans 15:2

Do you ever find yourself trying to get to the front of the line or into the front seat of the car? Many of us struggle sometimes with focusing on doing what's best for ourselves and not truly considering the needs of others. The thing you want might be good for you, but might not be good for your friend, family member, or classmate. And in some situations, that choice might actually lead to pain and hurt in your relationships rather than the harmony God desires.

It's easy to adopt a "me first" mentality in the culture we live in. We are quick to look out for what's best for ourselves rather than what's truly helpful to those around us. Paul wrote to the Christians in Rome, encouraging them to put others first in the matter of which foods they felt they had the right to eat.

We don't worry too much today about which food is appropriate for us to eat, but it's critical for us to consider whether our actions bring good to others or only to ourselves. God calls us to build others up by considering what is best for them, not simply what is best for us.

delight

Have you ever made a decision that you later realized wasn't good for those around you even though it might have been good for you? How did that make you feel?

Why do you think God wants us to seek good for others?

display

The next time you find yourself facing a decision that might impact those around you, pause. Slow down and try to see how that decision will affect the people in your life. Will it bring good to them? Or will it bring the harm or difficulty? Doing something for another's good may be more difficult on you, but just because something is difficult doesn't mean it isn't the right thing to do. Choose today to intentionally live with others' best interests in mind.

Take time to pray through any choices you may be currently facing. Ask God to give you wisdom in how those choices will impact other people. Seek to see situations with the same eyes God sees them with. Surrender to the Holy Spirit's control as He directs you to what is truly good for others.

Set Apart

LIFE IN THE LIGHT

- -

discover |

READ EPHESIANS 5:6-14.

For the fruit of the light consists of all goodness, righteousness, and truth...
—Ephesians 5:9

Were you ever scared of the dark as a kid? I was. I remember sleeping with my door partially open so I could see the hallway light. I remember needing my closet door to be fully closed so I wouldn't be afraid of what might be lurking inside. And I remember my imagination going wild with every distorted shape I could see in the dark bedroom. The funny thing, though, was how everything immediately changed when I turned on the light.

Before you knew Jesus, you lived in the darkness. But now, with Jesus, you live in the light. The problem for Christians comes when they live as if they are in darkness instead of living in the light. Walking in the light produces some key fruit: goodness, righteousness, and truth. This fruit cannot be produced while walking in darkness. It only comes from walking in the light.

There's no shame present when we walk in the light. We must simply walk in the reality that we are now children of light and not children of darkness. A changed life is the result of God bringing you into the light through Jesus. Today, you can remove the power that darkness has by focusing instead on being a child of the light.

delight

What are some of the main differences you see between a child of darkness and a child of the light?

How have you been tempted to slip into living in the old ways of darkness?

display

So, what do we do to walk in the light? First, we refuse to be deceived. It's critical to know and understand the truth God gives us through His Word. Second, we remember who we are. We are children of light. If you find yourself sliding into darkness, remind yourself of your identity as a child of the light. Finally, we expose the deeds of darkness instead of walking in them. The world of darkness has no power over you when you shine the light of truth on it.

Use your prayer time as an opportunity to reflect on your identity as a child of the light. Ask God to bring Scripture to mind that speaks to this new identity. Thank Him for rescuing you from the darkness. Commit to live with a new focus on your identity and not to be tempted by the darkness surrounding you in the world.

DESIRE FOR GOOD

- -

discover |

READ 2 THESSALONIANS 1:4-12.

In view of this, we always pray for you that our God will make you worthy of his calling, and by his power fulfill your every desire to do good and your work produced by faith, so that the name of our Lord Jesus will be glorified by you, and you by him, according to the grace of our God and the Lord Jesus Christ.
—2 Thessalonians 1:11-12

I hated salad when I was a kid. Actually, I hated everything about salad except for tomatoes. I would pick the tomatoes out of the salad my mom made every night and I would only eat those while avoiding the rest of the ingredients. Something amazing happened, though, as I grew older. I began to like salad. Now I love it, and I've even been known to order salad as my entire meal sometimes. Our taste in and desire for food has a tendency to change over the years.

As followers of Jesus, our desires change as well. It may seem completely abnormal to want to do good when you first start growing in your faith. But as the Holy Spirit transforms your character, you'll find that your desires change. One of those desires is the desire to do good. Even with that new desire, it can sometimes still be a challenge, which is why God is the One who empowers you to be able to fulfill that desire. Today, discover how God will provide you with the strength you need to live out this new desire. And maybe eat a salad.

delight |

How have you seen your desires change in a positive way since giving your life to Jesus and becoming a Christian?

Has it ever felt difficult to do good even when you wanted to? Why do you think that is?

display |

A mark of a growing Christian is an increasing desire to live God's way and to do good for others. You might need to check your heart if you are not seeing this desire increasing. Maybe there's something holding you back, like an unhealthy relationship, a sinful pattern of thinking, or even just the busyness of life.

Commit yourself today to seek God in a fresh way as you attempt to live by His power. Don't allow yourself to fall into a pattern of trying to do good on your own. It's only possible as He gives you the desire, grows that desire, and then empowers that desire.

Ask God to give you a fresh desire to do good. Admit your need for His power to accomplish good. Confess any times when you've tried to accomplish good on your own, apart from His strength.

FILLED WITH GOODNESS

- -

discover |

READ LUKE 6:43-49.

A good person produces good out of the good stored up in his heart. An evil person produces evil out of the evil stored up in his heart, for his mouth speaks from the overflow of the heart.
—Luke 6:45

Have you ever walked up to an apple tree and picked an orange, or walked up to a lemon tree and picked a plum? We all know how crazy it sounds to pick fruit off a tree that doesn't match the type of tree it is. Apple trees produce apples and lemon trees produce lemons.

In the same way, good people produce good fruit and bad people produce bad fruit. The key to producing good fruit isn't found in trying harder. The good fruit comes from our lives when our hearts are filled with goodness through the Holy Spirit.

So, how does someone become filled with goodness? Jesus illustrated this when He talked about building your life on a solid foundation of rock. The solid foundation comes when you take what Jesus taught and actually put it into practice. Jesus isn't looking for followers who simply hear what He says. He's looking for followers who will do what He says. Today, focus on how you can build your life on Jesus and follow His commands.

delight |

What do you think are some examples of fruit that are produced from the life of a good person?

How have you seen God produce fruit through your life?

display |

What does the fruit of your life look like? Take a deep look inside your heart and truly reflect on the type of fruit that comes out of your life. Think about whether it's fruit that points people to Jesus or points them away from Him. The most important thing you can focus on in life is developing a heart that's committed to Jesus's teachings and obeying them.

In order to obey the teachings of Jesus, you first need to know them. Spend time every day reading at least a little bit of the Bible. Ask God each day to give you insight into His Word. As you get to know these teachings better, commit to living them out through your actions each day. Then, you'll be filled with goodness through the power of the Holy Spirit.

Spend a few moments in reflective prayer. Ask God to show you what the true state of your heart is. Ask Him to reveal areas that need to line up more with who He's calling you to be. Surrender to all that God asks you to do and commit to live out His teachings with a good heart today.

DO WHAT IS GOOD

- -

discover |

READ 1 PETER 3:8-12.

*For the one who wants to love life and to see good days, let him keep his
tongue from evil and his lips from speaking deceit, and let him turn away
from evil and do what is good. Let him seek peace and pursue it, because
the eyes of the Lord are on the righteous and his ears are open to their
prayer. But the face of the Lord is against those who do what is evil.*
— 1 Peter 3:10-12

Life is full of "if/then" situations. If you drive over the speed limit,
then you will get a ticket. If you leave cookies in the oven too long,
then they will burn and taste terrible. If you don't study for your
math test, then your grade will suffer.

Today's passage contains a similar situation. If you do what is good,
then God will have His eyes on you and hear your prayers. If you
do what is evil, then His face will be against you. It's important to
note that our approval before God comes only through Jesus, but
because of our new life in Christ, the result is righteousness and
God's response described here in 1 Peter.

The passage also gives a simple list of what to do and what not to
do. The life of a good person is marked by things like sympathy
and love for one another. The life of an evil person is marked by
things like insulting others when they insult you.

Is it your goal to live in goodness? If so, look closely today at what
God is telling you through His Word.

delight |

How would you describe the differences between the actions of a good person and an evil person, described here in 1 Peter?

What does it look like for you to turn away from evil and do what is good?

display |

The good person's life is marked by doing no evil. Here's what happens as you continue to grow in your walk with Jesus: you'll discover a greater desire to do good and a greater hatred of doing what's evil. Don't hear this wrong. You will always wrestle with temptation, but the deeper your relationship goes with Jesus, the more you will find an ever-increasing desire to do what's good.

Have you been allowing evil into parts of your life? Decide today to take a turn in the opposite direction. Choose what's good instead of what's evil. Remember that God is ready to hear your prayer as you continue to pursue Him.

Take some time in prayer to meditate on the actions Peter described, both good and evil. Ask God to show you an area to either begin pursuing or to turn away from. Commit that area to the Lord as He gives you the strength to make a change.

LOVE YOUR ENEMIES

- -

discover |

READ MATTHEW 5:43-48.

But I tell you, love your enemies and pray for those who persecute you, so that you may be children of your Father in heaven. For he causes his sun to rise on the evil and the good, and sends rain on the righteous and the unrighteous.
—Matthew 5:44-45

It's easy to love people who are nice to you. No great feat is accomplished when you act loving toward your friends who treat you well. It isn't hard to show love to your brother or sister when they're being kind. But it is difficult to love people who are mean or rude. These are people you might even think of as enemies.

Jesus flipped the common understanding of what it meant to love your neighbor. People at that time understood it to be about loving your neighbor, but hating your enemy. If we claim to be children of God, then we must love our enemies in the same way He's loved His enemies. In fact, He loved you while you were still in sin and an enemy of God.

As you think today about what it means to love your enemy, keep in mind that love isn't about a feeling. Loving someone means you do good to them. It's actively choosing to do what's best for someone else, even if they don't do it back in return.

delight |

What is your natural response when someone treats you badly?

Why do you think Jesus made such a big deal about loving our enemies?

display |

The call to love your enemies is one of the most challenging commands Jesus gives us. But at the same time, it's one of the clearest ways we can see God transforming our character to look more like Jesus. There's probably someone in your life that you might consider to be an enemy. Choose today to do good toward your enemy. Choose to love them when they're unloving. Choose to be a reflection of the love our Father has shown toward us.

It's easy to pray for people you care deeply about, but it's tough to pray for people who are tough to love. Next time you find yourself frustrated with someone in your life, you might be tempted to complain about them, vent your frustrations, or keep thinking about the situation in your mind. Instead, pray for them. You'll discover quickly that praying for your enemies transforms the way you feel about them and act toward them.

Take a few minutes to pray specifically for people who are tough to love. Pray for them by name. Ask God to bring blessings into their lives. Commit yourself to love people even when they may not love you back.

AUTHENTIC GOODNESS

----

discover |

READ MATTHEW 22:1-14.

"Go then to where the roads exit the city and invite everyone you can to the banquet." So those servants went out on the roads and gathered everyone they found, both evil and good. The wedding banquet was filled with guests.
—Matthew 22:9-10

Everyone loves a good story. There's nothing better than hearing a great storyteller bring things to life through his or her words. Jesus was a master storyteller and often used parables as a way to communicate spiritual truths.

In Matthew 22:1-14, Jesus gave a picture of the people of Israel—God's chosen people—who God had sent his messengers to. But the people of Israel rejected these messengers. Jesus described God's judgment on those who rejected the message. The Father, instead, broadly opened up the invitation to all people to be His chosen people, no matter their goodness before knowing Him.

The picture of a full wedding banquet is incredible, but it also came with a warning. One guest in the parable wasn't wearing the proper wedding clothes, and he was thrown out and punished. You can't fake a relationship with God. You may be able to fool your friends, your pastor, and even your parents, but you will never be able to fool God. He provides the proper wedding clothes by allowing each of us the opportunity to place our trust in Christ. Today, reflect on what an authentic faith looks like.

delight |

Why do you think the original invited wedding guests in the story responded the way they did?

How does our goodness show that we truly belong to God?

display |

You can never earn your way to salvation. There's no amount of religious rituals or good deeds that could earn God's approval. This is evident in today's passage when we see what happened to the guest who was not properly dressed for the wedding. You might be tempted to "fake it until you make it," but God sees through our attempts to appear to be something we are not.

The goodness your life displays is a gift from God. It shows that you belong to Him. Seek to live in a way that is grateful for how God has invited you to the greatest wedding banquet of all time.

Express a prayer of gratitude today. Thank God for including you in His invitation to know Him. Praise Him for including you in His chosen people. Remind yourself that it's only because of God's wide invitation that you can have the privilege of knowing Him now.

DAY 21

GOODNESS DOES, PART 1

- -

discover |

READ MATTHEW 25:14-30.

"His master said to him, 'Well done, good and faithful servant! You were faithful over a few things; I will put you in charge of many things. Share your master's joy.'"
—Matthew 25:21

That little jolt you get inside when someone congratulates you for a job well done is one of the best feelings. It's like getting the top grade on an assignment, hitting the winning home run, or cooking a great meal for your family. Can you imagine how incredible it would feel to hear God tell you that you've done a good job?

God gives different gifts, abilities, and resources to every Christian. It isn't about how much He's given you, but rather what you do with what you've been given. Got a talent for singing? You can use your gifts to lead others in worship. Have a gift in building things? You can use that to help spruce up a home for an elderly neighbor. The key is using what God has given you for His glory and to help accomplish His mission.

On the flip side, Jesus used strong words in this parable for the servant who simply hid away what he'd been given. This servant was described as wicked and lazy. The end result for that service (or lack thereof) was the opposite of what we'd hope to hear when everything is said and done. Today, decide to be a servant who is active in doing good through what God's given you.

delight |

Why did the last servant simply hide his gift away?

What keeps you from fully utilizing the gifts God has given you?

display |

Good and faithful. Aren't those two words you'd love to hear when you see Jesus face to face one day? The time to ensure this response is now. God has gifted you. He's given you a unique personality, abilities, life experience, and spiritual gifts, and He doesn't want you to waste them.

Be a Christian who puts your faith into action. You've been placed for a purpose at this particular time and in this particular place. God has gifted you so you can use those gifts. Think through all He's given you and find ways to use those things for God's glory. In the end, there will be nothing better than being congratulated on a job well done by your Creator.

Pray today that God would help you see clearly how He has gifted and equipped you for a purpose. Commit to discovering those gifts and putting them to good use. Ask God to give you a clear opportunity today to glorify Him by putting your gifts into action.

DAY 22

GOODNESS DOES, PART 2

- -

discover |

READ MATTHEW 25:31-46.

"Then he will also say to those on the left, 'Depart from me, you who are cursed, into the eternal fire prepared for the devil and his angels! For I was hungry and you gave me nothing to eat; I was thirsty and you gave me nothing to drink; I was a stranger and you didn't take me in; I was naked and you didn't clothe me, sick and in prison and you didn't take care of me.'"
—*Matthew 25:41–43*

In the Scripture for today, Jesus continued the theme from earlier in Matthew 25. In this passage, Jesus highlighted how people who took care of those in need were actually taking care of Him. However, the opposite was also true. Those who didn't care for others in need had actually neglected Jesus. He referred to this second group of people as goats.

This passage gives us some insight into the earlier part of Matthew 25. Why did the man who buried the talent get cast out? He was like the goats in today's passage. He looked the part of a believer, but he clearly didn't believe. His life and actions didn't match up with what he'd said.

True followers of Christ is known by their actions. God's goodness overflows through them as they love people who others might overlook. Today, decide to be a follower of Jesus who lives out what you say you believe.

delight |

Why did Jesus tell the people in Matthew 25:41-43 to depart from Him? How do you think the people felt when they heard these words from Jesus?

Why is it so important that our actions match our beliefs?

display |

God's goodness is designed to show up in the way we live. The natural response for a believer when he or she sees a hurting person is to do whatever he or she can to meet that need. God has a huge heart for people who the world sees as the least. God is calling you to have that same heart for people.

You can discover all sorts of ways to minister to people who are hurting. You can ask your parents to go with you to visit sick people from your church, get some friends together to serve in a local homeless shelter in your city, or you can collect canned food to give to people who are in need. The bottom line is this: Christians see needs and seek to meet them. How will you meet them today?

During your time of prayer, ask God to give you a bigger heart for the least, the lost, and the left out. Seek His direction for how to personally get involved with helping those who need ministry in this way. Ask for open eyes to see the needs you might overlook every day.

DAY 23

EAGER TO DO GOOD

- -

discover |

READ TITUS 2:11-14.

He gave himself for us to redeem us from all lawlessness and to cleanse
for himself a people for his own possession, eager to do good works.
—Titus 2:14

If you're like most students, you probably have some
responsibilities at home that you don't exactly love doing. Maybe
it's taking out the trash, mowing the lawn, or unloading the
dishwasher. In fact, if you acted overly excited about any of those
tasks, the rest of your family might look at you like you were crazy.
Can you imagine being eager to do chores around the house?

But that's exactly what God calls us to when it comes to doing
good works. We shouldn't serve in ministry or help people out just
because it's what we're supposed to do. Instead, we should have
an attitude that's eager to do those things. Imagine jumping at the
opportunity to serve and do good for others!

God has rescued you through Christ not just so that you can be
free from sin, but so you would be eager to do good works. He's
creating a people who find absolute joy in the act of serving others
and putting the needs of others before their own.

delight |

In verse 12, what has God instructed us to avoid because of our salvation?

In the same verse, what has God commanded us to do in the place of the things to avoid?

display |

You weren't saved so you could just sit, attend church, and be with other Christians. Those things are important, but the purpose of your salvation is much bigger than that. You've been called to develop a heart that's eager to do good works.

How eager are you to do good works?

1	2	3	4	5	6	7	8	9	10
Nope.				**Meh.**					**For sure!**

It's easy to sometimes get into a rut of doing good just because it's what we're supposed to do out of some sense of duty. The next time you help someone out or serve in ministry, ask God to give you a fresh sense of eagerness. Spend time thinking about your attitude as you serve. If change is needed, decide to start developing the heart you know God wants you to have.

Spend a moment in prayer praising God for the gift of salvation. Thank Him for what He's saved you from. Ask Him to remind you that He's saved you for good works. If your attitude toward good works hasn't been great, ask God to give you a renewed sense of eagerness toward good works.

Set Apart

ROMANS 12:1-2

Therefore, I urge you, brothers and sisters, in view of God's mercy, to offer your bodies as a living sacrifice, holy and pleasing to God—this is your true and proper worship. Do not conform to the pattern of this world, but be transformed by the renewing of your mind. Then you will be able to test and approve what God's will is— his good, pleasing and perfect will.

THREE GOOD THINGS

- -

discover |

READ MICAH 6:8.

Mankind, he has told each of you what is good and what it is the LORD requires of you: to act justly, to love faithfulness, and to walk humbly with your God.

Imagine you got a job working at a local fast food restaurant (or maybe you already have one!). They'll spend some time teaching you how to work the equipment and the proper way to interact with customers. Chances are they'll hand you a job description—a written list of what's expected of you as an employee. Wouldn't it be great if all of life had a list of expectations like this?

In Micah 6:8, we're given three simple tasks that fulfill what God requires of us as His people. First, we're to act justly. This means treating others fairly, telling the truth, and speaking out on behalf of those who can't speak for themselves. Second, we're to love faithfulness. God calls you to faithfully obey Him in all His commands, showing your heart's commitment to faithfulness. Finally, we're to walk humbly with God. Our walk is a close relationship with God, but we also need to pursue it in humility. A humble walk means keeping a clear view of who God is and who you are in relationship to Him.

Today, let's dig in to the idea of what it looks like to follow God's expectations. Even though these seem simple, there's much to explore here. You just might discover an area where you need to do some growing.

delight |

Which of these three commands is the most difficult for you? Why?

Which of the three comes easiest for you? Why?

display |

Act justly. Love faithfulness. Walk humbly with your God. These three simple expectations summarize what it looks like to follow God. At the same time, even though they're simple, it will take you an entire lifetime to explore what it means to live these out. As you live out these commands, people will see a difference in your life. A changed life points people to Jesus.

How's your walk? As you live out what you've discovered today, make sure to look for opportunities to put these three things into practice. Pick one that may need a little attention and focus on living it out.

Take a few minutes of quiet prayer. Ask God to show you how to live out this verse. Repent of any areas where you haven't been living it out. Commit to growing in each of these areas.

Set Apart

DAY 25

KNOW WHAT IS GOOD

- -

discover

READ ROMANS 12:1-2.

Therefore, brothers and sisters, in view of the mercies of God, I urge you to present your bodies as a living sacrifice, holy and pleasing to God; this is your true worship. Do not be conformed to this age, but be transformed by the renewing of your mind, so that you may discern what is the good, pleasing, and perfect will of God.

What do you picture when you hear the word "worship"? You might picture things like a church service, singing, or maybe reading Scripture. All of those things are absolutely a part of worship, but worship is actually much bigger than that. Paul told the church in Rome that worship is actually about presenting ourselves as a living sacrifice.

Sacrifices in the Bible were typically an animal that was killed and offered to God. But a living sacrifice goes even further. Someone seeking to be a living sacrifice has to make a daily choice to surrender to God's way instead of his or her own way. A living sacrifice isn't influenced by the culture, but is instead transformed by a changed, or renewed, mind.

As you continue in this process of transformation, you're able to see clearly the good, pleasing, and perfect will of God. If you need clarity with a decision, the first place to start is by allowing your mind to be changed into God's way of thinking. In your time today, start this process of transformation as you dig into God's Word.

delight |

How is a living sacrifice different from a dead sacrifice?

How can you allow God to renew your mind and transform you?

display |

Everyone wants to know God's will for their lives, but it's not as mysterious as you might think. The key to knowing God's will starts with changing the way you think and see things. The process of being a living sacrifice daily and being transformed daily allows you to see God's point of view much more clearly. You won't ever understand everything, but you'll be able to know what good things to do next.

Here are a couple of questions for you: Are you regularly being a living sacrifice and are you regularly allowing God to renew your mind? It won't happen apart from spending time in the Bible and prayer. Carve out time each day for this important process.

As you pray today, focus on the idea of surrender. A living sacrifice requires giving up your own desires and replacing them with God's desires. Surrender to His will rather than your flesh. Surrender to God's way of thinking instead of your own. Ask God to renew your mind daily so you can be transformed.

Set Apart

DAY 26

IMITATE THE GOOD

- -

discover |

READ 3 JOHN 1:11.

Dear friend, do not imitate what is evil, but what is good. The one who does good is of God; the one who does evil has not seen God.

I love getting a good deal. I'm one of those people at the grocery store who will compare different brands and do the math to figure out which one offers the best value. The result of this approach is that I often walk away with a generic brand, which turns out to be merely a cheap imitation of the real thing.

Imitation sounds like a bad thing to us sometimes, but most of us imitate things around us even if we hate to admit it. In 3 John, the apostle encouraged us to think carefully about what we imitate. It's quick and easy to imitate what's evil because it's what we see around us in the world all day. It takes intentional effort to imitate what's good.

If you want to know someone's true character, look at whether they consistently imitate evil or good. None of us are perfect, and we will all sin at times. But the pattern of our lives ought to be one of choosing to imitate good, showing that we truly belong to God. Today, reflect on what you're imitating with your life.

delight |

What does a life that primarily imitates evil look like?

What does a life that primarily imitates good look like?

display |

How do you figure out what imitating good looks like? Start with Scripture. The Bible is full of instruction and examples of how to imitate what is good. You might also find a Christian who's been following Jesus a little while longer than you have. It's helpful to see faith lived out in real life so you can imitate it.

The next step of imitating good is realizing that other people look to your life to figure out what imitating good looks like. As you grow in your faith, look for a younger believer who you can help grow in his or her faith. You won't be the only example in his or her life, but you can be one important person who helps him or her see what it looks like to follow Jesus in a meaningful way.

> Pray today that God would open your eyes to what the Bible says about imitating good. Ask God to show you mentors in your life who can help you see how to live out the Bible's teachings. Surrender your heart to God as He prepares you to be an influence in the lives of others.

CLING TO GOOD, PART 1

- -

discover |

READ ROMANS 12:9-10.

Let love be without hypocrisy. Detest evil; cling to what is good.
—Romans 12:9

You've probably met someone who tried to be loving and friendly, but came across as fake. They smile to your face and may tell you that it's great to see you, but you can still pick up on something being off. Paul challenged us to love without hypocrisy. Our love for others is to be an honest and open type of love. This love for others is truly the opposite of evil.

The apostle Paul often gave a good replacement when he told us to avoid bad behavior. The replacement behavior here for detesting evil is to cling to what is good. In the context of this passage, this is lived out in our love for others. We're to love one another in a deep way—even as brothers and sisters. As a Christian, your spiritual family takes on an importance similar to the family you're born into.

Love is shown deeply to others primarily by how we treat them. We're to honor one another. This type of honor requires putting the needs of others above our own, treating people with respect, and always assuming the best in them. Today, focus on how you can find new ways to cling to what is good by the way you love other people, and especially other Christians.

delight |

What does it look like to love without hypocrisy?

Why is it important to view other Christians as our brothers and sisters?

display |

Evil and good are complete opposites of each other. You can't be pursuing what is good while slightly dabbling in what is evil. This is why Paul made it so clear that we are to detest evil and cling to good. Detest is another word for hate. How is your hatred of evil? We're not necessarily talking about evil in others, but in you. Do you hate it when you give in to sin?

On that same note, how are you doing at clinging to what is good? Clinging to what is good is more than acting a certain way at church and another way at school. Picture someone clinging to the side of a cliff while rock climbing. The climber is going to use every ounce of his or her energy to cling on to what he or she can. Your pursuit of good should have that same type of intensity. Make a determination to fully cling to what is good by how you treat others.

In your prayer time, ask God to give you an ever-increasing desire to cling to what is good. Repent of any times you've dabbled with evil rather than detesting it. Pray that God would show you opportunities to love others deeply.

CLING TO GOOD, PART 2

- -

discover |

READ ROMANS 12:11-15.

Do not lack diligence in zeal; be fervent in the Spirit; serve the Lord.
—Romans 12:11

The process of clinging to what is good is essential for growing in our walk with God. In today's passage, Paul gave a series of short commands that really help us figure out what it looks like to cling to good.

- Be fervent in the Spirit. Paul encouraged Christians to have a passion and enthusiasm for their faith. People get enthusiastic about their favorite singer, college football team, or hobby. But what if that same level of enthusiasm was directed by the Holy Spirit? This type of enthusiasm would be centered on the things of God rather than the things of this world.

- Serve the Lord. Walking in the Spirit will lead to a passion to serve God. Your faith needs to have a place to flow out of your life, not just be in a state of always receiving. If you find you don't have a desire to serve the Lord, maybe it's time to reexamine your walk with God and reconnect with Him in a fresh way.

Look closely at the other short commands Paul gave in this passage. You'll find encouragement there to pray, rejoice, share, and more. Each of these is a critical part of clinging to good.

delight |

**Take a look through the list of commands in Romans 12:11-15.
Which is one you need to work on?**

**Which command could you help another Christian grow in?
Who will you help?**

display |

The process of clinging to good is completely tied to the resulting actions in our lives. In other words, as you cling to what is good, it will change the way you live and treat other people. It's difficult to bless those who persecute you. It's challenging to be patient in affliction. It's not always easy to be hospitable to others, but the life of a follower of Jesus is marked by these things. Put these commands into practice today, even if you don't feel like it. Create new habits of how you treat others that will ultimately shape your life and character.

Take some time to pray. Focus on one or two of the commands in this passage and ask God for His help in living them out. Confess your need for His strength as you recognize you can't do this alone.

CLING TO GOOD, PART 3

- -

discover |

READ ROMANS 12:16-18.

If possible, as far as it depends on you, live at peace with everyone.
—*Romans 12:18*

My two daughters have been known to occasionally argue and fight. I'm sure you've exeprienced this if you have siblings. One thing I'm constantly telling my daughters is to not worry about what the other person did or is doing. Instead, I encourage them to focus on their response to the situation and how they can change their own actions.

In continuing our theme of clinging to good, Paul gave a great piece of wisdom: we're to live at peace with everyone. But he included an important note: "as far as it depends on you." It's impossible for you to control the actions of others or how they respond to different situations in life. But you can control how you respond to them and how you treat them. You may have a friend who's been treating you poorly. You can't fix what they've done, but you can choose to treat them with kindness and to not stir up any more issues than are already there.

Today, think about the part you play in keeping harmony in the different relationships in your life. You can't control everything that happens, but you can make some key choices that will help you live at peace with everyone.

delight |

Why is it not always possible to live at peace with everyone?

What are some ways you think Christians can make a better effort to live at peace with everyone?

display |

You do not have complete control over the health of every relationship you're in. You really don't have any control over how other people act in relationships. But you do have control over how you act in relationships and how you respond to conflict.

How do you respond when a friend or family member treats you poorly? Do you blow up in anger? Do you retreat and get silent? Choose today to respond with God's love as best as you're able. Don't forget that you have the Holy Spirit living in you, and He will empower you to love others even when it's hard.

Ask God to reveal relationships to you that may need a greater effort on your part to live at peace. Confess any ways you may have contributed to the conflict in the relationship. Commit to approaching those relationships differently.

CONQUER EVIL WITH GOOD

- -

 discover |

READ ROMANS 12:19-21.

Do not be conquered by evil, but conquer evil with good.
—Romans 12:21

You've probably heard the saying, "Don't get mad. Get even." This is terrible advice! Our natural reaction when someone hurts us is to get back at them. We may even want to hurt them slightly worse than they hurt us, but this type of approach never ends well.

First, Paul made it clear in this passage that vengeance, or getting back at someone, is not your job. Vengeance belongs to God. You must remember that God will one day set everything right that has been made wrong. So when we choose to return evil with evil, we're forgetting our place in the big picture. Our role isn't to bring punishment on others. God will determine where judgment is needed and what it will look like.

Second, instead of repaying evil with evil, you can choose a completely different approach. Paul said your approach ought to be repaying evil with good. This approach makes no sense to our culture. Our culture encourages us to get back at people when they hurt us. Instead, Christians are commanded to simply bring blessings upon people when they hurt us.

Today, determine to hear these words of Scripture with fresh ears. Listen to what God is saying through Paul. You may find some relationships in your life in which you've been hoping for revenge, but can now choose a different approach.

delight |

Why is it important to recognize that vengeance belongs to God instead of us?

What is one way you can choose to conquer evil with good?

display |

The act of seeking vengeance when you're hurt is never helpful. It may make you feel good in the moment, but it doesn't really accomplish anything. Plus, it tries to take over God's role in the situation. Think through relationships in your life where there may be some difficulties. Have you been trying to seek revenge in any of them?

It's tough to not seek revenge. The easy choice is to go for the cheap shot and seek vengeance on your own. Make the difficult choice to trust that God will do what's right when others have harmed you. This choice will be the best choice for both you and the person who's hurt you.

Take a few minutes in quiet prayer. If there are any relationships where someone has caused you hurt, now is the time to release that hurt. Give that hurt and pain to God instead of carrying it yourself. Surrender the desire to seek revenge and tell God of your trust in Him with all relationships in your life.

HE IS GOOD

How do we know that God is good? We sing about His goodness, we read in His Word that He is good, and when troubling situations arise, we often hear people say, "But God is still good!" While all of these things are true, have you ever stopped to think about what it really means to say that God is good?

Describe what you mean when you say God is good or what you think when you hear someone else say God is good.

Maybe some of our uncertainty over the question "Is God good?" can be attributed to the overuse and misunderstanding of the word in general. When we think "good," we might think: "Well, it's so-so, but it's isn't awesome." Or we may think of good as something that is favorable, thriving, attractive, unharmed/OK, sound, not expired, pleasant, or witty.[1]

How would you describe your standard for good?

When you think about God being good, does this come from your own personal standard for good? Or do you believe God exists above and beyond what we could define as good? Explain.

Read Exodus 33; 34:6; Nehemiah 9:20; Psalm 27:13; 145:9; Mark 10:18; and James 1:17. What would you change about your definition of God's goodness after reading these verses? Why?

Here's the thing: God isn't "good" by comparison to something or someone else. He isn't good because He lives up to (or obliterates) our personal standards for goodness. His goodness isn't harsh, uncaring, or any other negative argument people make against God's goodness. It's not even His holiness, mercy, or ethical standard—though those things are true.

God's goodness flows from His character as the one true God, who is never in need, but, instead, constantly gives to the ones He created. His goodness encompasses His kindness, generosity, and the overall joy He brings to the world He so deeply loves. His goodness is necessary because it is a part of His character. But He doesn't have to be good to us—He chooses to. And God wants us to know Him and enjoy His goodness! He expresses this time and time again in His Word and in His actions.[2]

Think about it: God loves us so deeply and so intensely desires us to experience His goodness that a holy God made a way for a sinful world to be forgiven. And the way wasn't painless, but required the sacrifice of His only Son to bring death to sin and victory over the grave so that we might have a relationship with Him. Every second, He extends an invitation for us to come and enjoy "the Lord's goodness in the land of the living" (Ps. 27:13).

Describe how your definition of God's goodness has changed throughout this devotional.

BEFORE I STARTED   **AFTER I FINISHED**

I KNEW ALL ALONG

WHAT IT TAKES TO BE GOOD

As we know, everyone has a different definition of what's "good," so it should come as no surprise that the idea of what makes a person good varies, too. While you may be ready to spout off the church answer of "It's Jesus," just hold onto that thought for a minute. While that answer is correct, have you ever considered the backing for it? Do you know how to support the idea that Jesus is the ONLY one who makes us good in a sinful culture filled with competing ideas about what "good" really is?

Let's start by taking a look at some common cultural beliefs about what it means to be "good." Then, we'll take a look at what God's Word says is true. For each option, color, shade, or highlight the icon that most accurately represents your view: thumbs up icon (if you agree), or the thumbs down icon (if you disagree).

You're a good person if ...

 1. You're a rule follower. You don't steal or cheat, and you try to always tell the truth.

 2. You have a "moral compass" and you stick to your beliefs while respecting others.

 3. Those closest to you—your friends, family, small group members, classmates, and so on—can describe you as someone who has solid character.

 4. You're not arrogant or too stuck on yourself. You're compassionate and considerate of others.

 5. You're neither too objective nor too emotional. You look at all the facts before making a decision, but you balance that by considering feelings, too.[3]

How do these statements align with what you already know about God, His Word, His goodness, and His plan for us?

Truthfully, Scripture describes us—humanity as a whole—as sinful. But what does that mean?

- *Merriam-Webster* defines sin as "an offense against religious or moral law; an action that is or is felt to be highly reprehensible; an often serious shortcoming."[4]

- The *Holman Illustrated Bible Dictionary* says that sin is any action "by which humans rebel against God, miss His purpose for their life, and surrender to the power of evil rather than to God."[5]

Put simply, sin is unrighteousness or going against God's good design for us. Even though the cultural definition doesn't say that explicitly; the actions listed as sin are still not God's best for us. These definitions reveal what is "bad" or wrong, but both also clearly point to what they believe to be the solution:

- Don't disobey the religious/moral law you follow. Don't do anything that others would find worthy of judgment. Work on ironing out your flaws.

- Follow God and His Word. Pursue His purpose for your life. Give your life fully to Him.

From our culture's vantage point, we are in control—we just need to work on being the best version of ourselves, whatever that happens to be in the court of popular opinion. From a biblical perspective, we are completely unable to make ourselves good because we are sinful and unrighteous. But the good news is that God is able to make us good—He provided a way for us to be made holy and righteous through Jesus.

The world tells us we're good by what we do and based on our character, but God says we're good because of what He's done for us and based on His character. So, we are not saved because we are good. We are saved because He is good. We are saved from ourselves, for Him (to be His children), and for the good works He has planned for us.

A MEASURE OF GOOD

Briefly review the actions our culture says make someone a good person on pages 74-75, then take a few minutes to complete the following. Rate how "good" each action is on a scale of 1 to 10, with one being "nothing good here," five being "eh, anyone would do that," and 10 being "wow, that's amazing!"

Maddie does her best to refrain from gossip, foul language, and making suggestive jokes.

1   2   3   4   5   6   7   8   9   10

Allen tries not to put himself in situations where he's alone with a girl and keeps parental locks on his phone and computer so he doesn't see graphic images.

1   2   3   4   5   6   7   8   9   10

Instead of going out with friends on Friday nights, Leilani helps provide childcare at her church for attendees of an addiction recovery program.

1   2   3   4   5   6   7   8   9   10

At least once a week, Sam's mom takes him to visit with an elderly widow from their church. They spend hours together, baking cookies and talking about life.

1   2   3   4   5   6   7   8   9   10

Keisha donates her old clothes, shoes, and purses to a clothing closet in her community that provides for the poor.

1   2   3   4   5   6   7   8   9   10

Although each of these are good—and biblical (see Prov. 1:17; 1 Cor. 6:18; Phil. 2:4; Eph. 4:29-31; and Jas. 1:27)—things we can do for others, the actions in and of themselves are not good or what make us good. They aren't what saves us, either. We've already discussed God's goodness and what it means for us to be "good," but we have to take a deeper look at what it means to be saved for good works, not by them.

We frequently hear the mantra in our culture of: You are enough. As an encouragement to be who God created you to be, and that you don't have to be and do everything, this holds up. But it doesn't quite translate into our spiritual lives. The harsh reality here is that we could never measure up to God's standard of holiness or be "good enough" on our own. Thankfully, alongside this difficult truth is a grace beyond our comprehension: Jesus's perfect life and sacrifice for us was, is, and always will be good enough. To have a relationship with God, we don't have to be perfect; we just have to have Jesus.

> We don't have to be perfect
> to have a relationship with God,
> we just have to have Jesus.

NOTES

NOTES

ENDNOTES

1 "Good," accessed March 23, 2021, https://www.merriam-webster.com/dictionary/good.

2 Kevin DeYoung, "The Goodness of God," The Gospel Coalition, April 20, 2020, https://www.thegospelcoalition.org/blogs/kevin-deyoung/the-goodness-of-god/.

3. Ronald E Riggio, "How Can You Tell If You Are a Good Person?," Psychology Today (Sussex Publishers, October 14, 2016), https://www.psychologytoday.com/blog/cutting-edge-leadership/201610/how-can-you-tell-if-you-are-good-person?eml.

4. "Sin," Merriam-Webster (Merriam-Webster), accessed March 25, 2021, https://www.merriam-webster.com/dictionary/sin.

5. Chad Brand et al., "Sin," in Holman Illustrated Bible Dictionary (Nashville, TN: Holman Reference, 2015).